CRYSTAL READINGS

by Rebecca Steele

Copyright © 2017 Rebecca Steele. All rights reserved. No part of this book may be reproduced, stored in a retrieval system, or transmitted in any form or by any means, electronic, mechanical, photocopying, recording, or otherwise, without the prior written permission of the Copyright owner.

Published 2017

ISBN 978-0-646-96980-0

Publishing services by Gunn & Penn Press

Global distribution services by Ingram Spark

facebook.com/RebeccaSteeleCrystals

None of the ideas, rituals or suggested practices contained in this book should be used as a substitute for professional medical treatment. Please consult a medical practitioner. This book is for entertainment purposes only. No responsibility can be accepted for any loss, injury or inconvenience sustained by any person, business, or organization using this book for any reason.

For all old souls and their burdens

choosing crystals

There are hundreds of different crystals and they come in a kaleidoscope of colors and forms. This can sometimes be overwhelming when trying to decide which ones to buy.

In this book, 68 crystals are identified as keystones for crystal readings, although you can always add others depending on which you are drawn too.

The rule of thumb is that crystals choose you. When shopping for crystals, be aware when drawn to a particular crystal and stay open-minded when browsing.

size

A crystal's ability is not determined by size. Some of the smallest stones will demonstrate energy equal to larger stones. However, smaller tumbled stones are the most useful for readings.

imperfections

Some crystals have imperfections that have special meanings such as phantoms where a crystal appears to be set inside another crystal which is highly prized in things such as quartz. Other imperfections such as depressions or keyholes also indicate higher meanings and add the crystal's elemental ability. For this reason, it is best to view a crystal from all sides and to hold it in your hand, hold it up to the light and feel its weight.

rough or polished

Crystals can be rough, polished and clustered and come in a variety of shapes. Tumbled and polished crystals provide the most convenience for everyday use and are the most common. Polished crystals are simply rough crystals that have been placed in a tumbler with a special medium such as crushed walnut shells, to remove the rough edges and provide the smooth polished surface.

Roughs are in their most natural form and can sometimes be useful when looking for increased energy. They often lack the beauty of polished crystals but are of the same metaphysical value.

imitations

Some stones sold as crystals are nothing more than manufactured colored glass or heat treated crystals of lesser value. For example, stones such as obsidian can often be purchased in a variety of unnatural colors including pink and blue. These are most likely simply manufactured colored glass.

Some crystals are branded and sold under a trade name. Bolivianite, which is actually a mix of amethyst and citrine, is an example and may communicate elements that are different to those expected.

It's recommended that you determine the authenticity of crystals to ensure you are buying good stones. A reputable seller should always state whether the stone is natural, treated or manufactured. If in doubt, always ask. Good sellers will be aware of the origins of their stones and very likely happy to tell you all about them.

categories

The 68 essential crystals are arranged in the following categories. Look for these symbols in the crystal listings for quick reference.

  Clearing - to remove obstacles and provide clear pathways

  Energizing - to provide energy to the desired outcomes

  Grounding - To gather knowledge or foster understanding

  Protecting - To safeguard the element or outcome

caring for crystals

Crystals are made up of naturally occurring minerals that have been fused together under enormous pressure and extreme heat, deep within the earth. It is worth remembering that most of today's crystals were formed thousands, if not millions of years ago and carry with them all of the history of the earth from which they were created.

No two crystals will be alike and the degradation or destruction of a crystal is final and will require it to be replaced. With this in mind, crystals should be treated as living objects and shown appropriate care.

scratching

Most crystals are fairly resilient to knocks and bumps, however, you should take care to avoid mixing rough stones with polished stones as this may cause chipping or scratches on the surface.

If a crystal is too scratched or becomes dull with use, replace it.

immersion

Some crystals will tolerate being immersed in liquids however others will not. Some are sensitive to water and may become cloudy, lose or change color or in some cases dissolve completely. Others can contain minerals that may be harmful with prolonged exposure or if consumed. For these reasons, immersing crystals for any purpose is not recommended.

As a rule, you should never need to immerse a crystal in any liquid unless it has become encrusted with dirt, in which case it should be replaced.

cleaning

With handling, crystals will pick up oils, which in turn will attract dirt and dust. To clean your crystals, wipe them over with a soft natural cloth, preferably cotton or flannel, dampened with ordinary tap water. Use warm water if required to remove oils. Never use commercial cleaning chemicals of any kind.

smudging

Where crystals have been exposed to negative energy or where a crystal's performance seems to have weakened, prepare a smudge bath by placing them on a cloth and passing a lit smudge stick over and around them. Use a feather to blow the smoke over them. This will draw out the negativity energy and carry it away in the smoke.

Smudge sticks are generally made of white sage and come in many sizes. They are readily available from most metaphysical shops or online. Ensure the herbs used have been gathered from a sustainable source and, where possible, prepared using Native American traditions. Be careful not to burn your crystals by placing them too close to the smudge or to candles as they may break.

keep it natural

The trick with crystal care is to keep it as simple and as natural as possible. This way your crystals should remain as new for many years. Look after them as they look after you.

activating crystals

Preparing your stones for readings is a fairly simple process. You can use them as they are, however you will get heightened power and energy from crystals that have been activated.

Setting your stones in sunlight for a time is a common method. A nice spot on a kitchen shelf will do. However, some crystals are sensitive to sunlight and you may see some colors fade if left sitting too long or exposed repeatedly.

The best method for programming or activating your crystals is to leave them exposed in the light of a full moon for a few hours. Make sure they are out of the weather and always try for times when the moon has fully risen and at its sharpest. While night time is usually best, sometimes the moon will be visible at its fullest during daylight hours. Choose what is most convenient for you.

Those who practice astrology may also energize certain crystals with reference to the planets viewable in the sky at the time.

Before and after activation, give your crystals a gentle wipe over to remove any traces of dirt and oils. Avoid using chemically impregnated cloths such as lens cleaners. Opt instead for a soft cotton or flannel cloth made damp with ordinary tap water.

From time to time, give your crystals a boost by repeating the activation process.

castings and layouts

How to cast crystals for readings depends on the depth of the reading to be undertaken. A short reading will only require a few crystals which can be interpreted quickly. More detailed readings can be undertaken by expanding the cast and making different layouts, giving more wide-ranging information.

the language of crystal readings

While crystals have been around for millennia and have a variety of uses, it is easy to try and place some degree of mysticism within the cast stones. However, crystal casts are for everyday purposes so therefore the language used should reflect everyday situations. Using "a long and arduous path to glorious ascension" when you really mean to say "going on a relaxing holiday" would be a good example.

As you learn the language of the stones, keep it simple and therefore meaningful.

interpreting the cast

Depending on how many stones are cast, they should be interpreted individually first and then in relation to the adjacent stones. For example, when goldstone appears in a cast it signifies a social gathering. When dumortierite is also present it can indicate the gathering will be work related whereas black onyx would indicate the gathering to be more family related or a journey home.

Also, look for a preponderance of stones such as a lot of energizing stones or clearing stones, etc. Similarly, the absence of a category may have other meanings.

As you learn to read crystals and become familiar with how their positions relate, you will be able to draw your own associations. Also, it will be useful to keep a notebook handy and jot down your interpretations as you go. This will help you to build up a body of knowledge and in time help your readings to become more fluid.

reading for yourself and other people

Casting for yourself can often be difficult as it is hard to remain objective. Often the advice of the crystals is tainted by your own hopes and dreams or a desire for specific outcomes. As you become more practiced and free your mind from the constraints of bias, the interpretation of your castings will become more relevant.

Reading for other people is much less cumbersome, especially if the reading is cold, that is you have no knowledge of the client's current or past situations. When starting out, it's best to advise others that you are testing the validity of your casts and ask for some feedback. You must however always be respectful of privacy.

layouts

simple 3 or double 3 cast

The simple 3 cast is quick and easy to interpret.

In this reading, a single crystal is cast into each of the spheres, representing the past events, the present situation, and the possible outcomes. If reading for a client, you can ask the client to position the stones, choosing from the 68 crystals at random.

Read each crystal in relation to which sphere it is in.

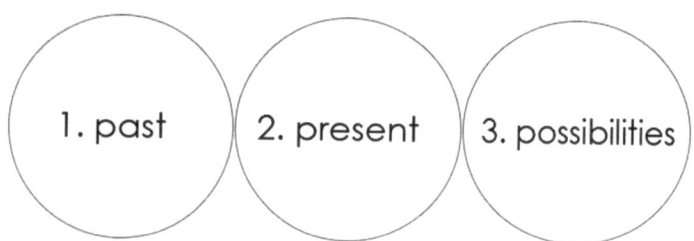

1st – the issue at the present. What has brought the client to this point?
2nd – what governs the issue. What needs to be done?
3rd – possible outcomes.

In the double 3, two crystals are placed in each sphere and are read in conjunction. The first of the two is the dominant factor, the latter is a supporting idea or hidden factor.

celtic cross cast

This cast is similar to the standard celtic cross spread used in the Tarot, with the addition of a soul stone.

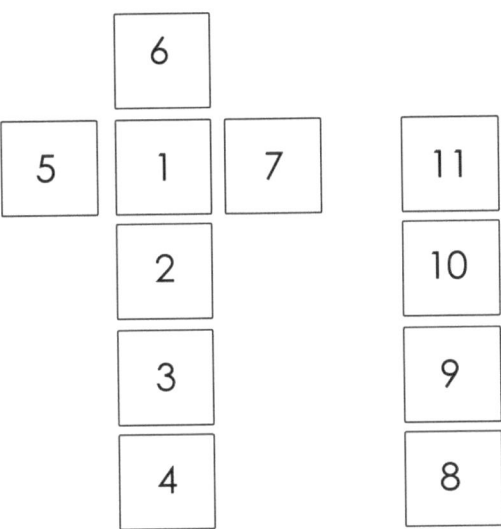

1.	soul	The state of the client's soul. Represents the basis of the question.
2.	underlying influence	What the major concern is
3.	further information	How the client feels about the situation
4.	foundation	How the situation came about
5.	past	What has happened in the past
6.	overlying influence	What is affecting the situation now
7.	immediate future	What is the way forward right now
8.	outside view	How others see the situation
9.	Internal hopes	What the client hopes will happen
10.	relationships	What other factors are involved
11.	outcome	How the situation will be resolved

life journey cast

1.	soul	The state of the individual for whom the cast is made
2.	energy	Path to stimulating and balancing energy flows
3.	awareness	Path to personal awareness development
4.	relationship	Path to love, friendships, and bonds
5.	higher	Connection with higher powers and influences
6.	meditation	Path to harmony and visualization
7.	material	Path to wealth and prosperity
8.	physical	Path to health and wellbeing
9.	emotional	Path to comfort and self-belief
10.	affirmation	Path to empowerment and peace
11.	wisdom	Connection with and retaining knowledge
12.	virtuous	Path to personality trait development
13.	protection	Path to safety and stability
14.	psychic	Mental power development and attunement
15.	unknown	Represents the unknowable

the 68 essential crystals

agate

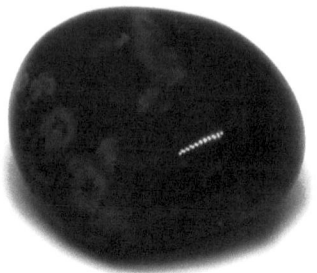

advantage

cast meaning

When agate appears in a cast it suggests the client is stuck in a rut of some sort, whether it's in a personal relationship, a job, home life or just life in general. There are no barriers preventing the client moving forward, it's just the client has not looked ahead, or beyond the current situation. There are advantages that are currently hidden from view.

path forward

Encourage the client to imagine different scenarios that alter the current position, enabling them to see things in a new light. This does not mean the position has to change, it means that applying a new positive attitude may reveal positive aspects to which the client is currently unaware.

outcomes

With a new or enhanced perception of a stagnant situation, the client is able to see things that currently exist and apply them in a new way, enabling them to take advantage of aspects that were previously unknown or ways unconsidered.

amazonite

self-reliance

cast meaning

Amazonite governs personal resolve. It not only helps to strengthen commitments, it also helps to find calm and order. The presence of amazonite indicates a personal belief or action is providing a strong influence which may be negative or positive. For example, the client may have a strong belief which is creating disorder.

path forward

The client would find benefit in either staying with beliefs if they are providing a positive influence (stay strong) or to use the time to calm a situation that is giving unrest (resolve to find strength). The client should recognize that strength comes from within and he/she cannot just rely on others to solve issues.

outcomes

Strong beliefs will help to overcome problems. With self-reliance, the client can build on strength to deal with issues as they arise. An "I can do it" attitude will positively influence all outcomes.

amethyst

creation

cast meaning

When amethyst appears in a cast there is a creative atmosphere surrounding the current situation. New things are happening, new ideas are being exchanged and processes formed. In extreme circumstances, it can be "out with the old and in with the new".

path forward

The client should be encouraged to participate in the creative process and not hold back in voicing ideas. Be open to the creative flow and listen to all contributions. Some old ideas will benefit from renovation.

outcomes

There are gains to be made from things created, new experiences that were previously unavailable and emotions that were dormant. All will help to move forward in a positive light.

ametrine

middle ground

cast meaning

Ametrine governs logic and the male influence. As a stone that is strongly grounded by balance, it is unaffected by emotions and reveals practical values in relationships and objects. Ametrine sees things as they really are, rather than how they are imagined to be. In all areas, it finds the comfortable middle ground.

path forward

The client is encouraged to find order. Making lists and methodically doing the items on the list will help the client to accomplish goals. It will also put the list in the background of life, becoming things they do rather than who they are. Ametrine will enhance and foster friendships and indicates that a broken relationship needs to be fixed. The presence of ametrine may also indicate a strong older male influence.

outcomes

The process of getting things in order will free up emotions to other influences such as happiness, inspiration, and motivation. A path to mending broken friendships will be found, as will happy mediums in areas of life that are conflicted.

apatite

revelation

cast meaning

When apatite appears in a cast there is concern over truth. There may be betrayal or deception involved in a situation. Apatite also represents forgiveness, suggesting that a lie is made without malice.

path forward

When the client is moving toward a goal, there is something he/she is not seeing. With blinkers on, the client may be subject to some hidden truth that could be detrimental when revealed. In this case, the client should take the time to investigate the details before making critical decisions, and before it creates conflict.

outcomes

Remaining in a state of suspicion will lead to regret. Failing to question will cause disadvantage. In revealing the truth, there is a forward path to reconciliation and forgiveness.

aquamarine

sixth sense

cast meaning

Aquamarine is the stone of the sixth sense and in a cast represents the greater unknown, the unknowable or that for which there isn't a single answer or solution. While aquamarine seems to provide the client with no information, it is really saying that information isn't available at this time, or there are so many possible solutions that it's impossible to predict which is best or which will occur.

path forward

When aquamarine appears in a cast, the client is encouraged to take whatever action feels best at the time, as all outcomes are possible. Rather than seeing this as a negative, the client should recognize that any choice will reveal more information and the client should trust their instincts - the forward path is unchartered territory. Any attempt to analyze will only result in remaining in the same position. The client may also be encouraged to develop their intuitive senses.

outcomes

This is a time of both curiosity and discovery. In following intuitive paths, greater heights or understanding will be reached and options revealed that will lead to a perfect outcome.

aventurine

triumph

cast meaning

Aventurine indicates the pursuit of a goal where the desired outcome is a triumph. In this, there is an expected finish line, upon which success can be measured. While aventurine can govern all pursuits, it is particularly related to things in the material world such as business ventures or financial matters.

path forward

Climbing the mountain may not be easy, however in perseverance success is available. If the client is working to attract financial abundance or material stability, and there is a distinct activity being undertaken to achieve this goal, then the client will be rewarded. Persistence is key although single-mindedness may cause the endeavor to fail. Other cast crystals may indicate obstacles such as impatience and delays.

outcomes

Hard work will be acknowledged and rewards will be reaped when the top of the mountain is reached.

black obsidian

courage

cast meaning

Black obsidian is directly related to fear and insecurity. Its appearance in a cast indicates the client is being held back and that apprehension is preventing them from making decisions and moving forward.

path forward

The client should be encouraged to turn and face fears head on, rather than looking back at what created the fear in the first place. This is the time to push through. When faced with many choices, there is hesitation and this will only affirm the fear, causing further insecurity. Black obsidian indicates the client can summon the courage to make decisions, even if the choice is scary.

outcomes

When fears are put aside, courage will lead to a joyous and successful outcome. The fear itself becomes less important.

black onyx

pilgrimage

cast meaning

Black onyx is the pilgrim's stone. It represents the place where ideas and attitudes are formed and we build things that remain with us throughout our lives. While sometimes, core values may be lost or clouded, it is possible for them to be found and rekindled.

path forward

When black onyx appears in a cast, the client is encouraged to take a journey home. This may not be the place of birth or the place where he/she was raised, in fact, it may not be a physical place at all. A pilgrimage represents taking a journey to a place where underlying beliefs and values were formed or possibly holds the beliefs and values the client wants to attain. If the client is unable to connect with their roots on a spiritual level, then a physical journey home should provide insights.

outcomes

In returning to roots, the source of both inspiration and healing can be found. There will be help and guidance available if they are asked for.

blue fluorite

interlude

cast meaning

When blue fluorite appears in a cast, it indicates that timeout is necessary in order to restore calm and rebalance life. It can also represent a holiday to be undertaken, or a relationship that has been broken is ready to be repaired.

path forward

The client is encouraged to step back for a while, especially if things are hectic or confused. He/she may have a feeling of being burnt out or that things have run their course. Taking a breather and using the time to re-energize will strengthen future activities. When dealing with broken ties or family issues specifically, the client can use this time to open communication.

outcomes

Time taken for rest will be both restorative and energizing and will help to revitalize the way forward.

blue quartz

comfort

cast meaning

Blue quartz governs comfort during periods of grief and loss, as well as self-esteem. It is highly attuned to emotions and indicates that some sadness or depression is creating unease. This leads to dissatisfaction with the current situation.

path forward

The client should understand that feeling sad during times of loss is normal and it should be allowed to run its course – the spirit will always try to return to joy, if even for a moment. The client may unable to block pain completely but is able to allow it time. Eventually, the feeling of grief will dissipate. However, if the client wallows in the pain for too long, never allowing the spirit to emerge, further problems can manifest, such as depression, isolation, and low self-esteem.

outcomes

While accepting the grieving process is just that – a process - unease is simply the necessary path the spirit must take. Pain is always temporary as we eventually revert to natural human instincts, and find comfort.

bronzite

fortitude

cast meaning

The client may be experiencing difficulty with a person such as a parent, child or partner, or an activity such as work. When bronzite appears in a cast it indicates that personal strength and support is available in any difficulty that requires concerted effort for a length of time. This may be in recovery from illness or addiction, or tasks that need sustained effort to complete.

path forward

When cast, encourage the client to use strength from within to sustain them through hard times. They should not rely on others to solve it for them, nor should they lean on some other person as a crutch, as this is only ever a temporary fix. The message is to never give up. They should persevere with what seems right, and also to stand up and defend beliefs, especially in their personal ability. By owning the problem, the client can overcome trouble.

outcomes

In drawing on internal fortitude, bad or damaging habits can be broken, strength will endure and grow, and new positive relationships will emerge. Never run away from anything. Always run toward something.

carnelian

acrimony

cast meaning

When carnelian appears in a cast it indicates that rage is having a negative influence. This rage is caused by events that are now in the past, but there is still a substantial amount of anger and resentment felt toward the issues.

path forward

The client should be encouraged to address the source of the anger rather than letting it manifest. Where this is impossible, the client should learn to direct the energy of acrimony in a more positive way, as anger is just negative energy that needs an escape route. Any route will do, it doesn't have to be in conflict with the source. This can be as small as finding something else to do that requires energy – even housework, or taking a walk. When all else fails, the client should give anger and resentment to a greater power, or to the universe.

outcomes

In dealing with anger we deal only with the energy it creates. If that energy is expelled in a positive way, the anger becomes just temporary and does no harm.

chalcedony

intellect

cast meaning

Chalcedony is the crystal of the mind, and like the mind, it signifies there are two distinct sides to an issue. One that is logical and methodical and one that is emotional and imaginative. When appearing in a cast, chalcedony signifies that a situation or issue is not understood and that only one side has been revealed. There are hidden truths, misconceptions and a lack of sound reasoning surrounding what is at stake.

path forward

The client is encouraged to look beyond the chatter. He/she has yet to form a real opinion based on either evidence or experience. Instead, the client is being led by others, giving value to gossip and misinformation. There is a lot to be learned by investigating the underlying issues, taking off the blinkers and hearing both sides of the story.

outcomes

Rather than adhering to a one-sided view which can lead us to jump to unfounded conclusions, a more balanced attitude can be found when pausing to discover both sides.

chrysoprase

prosperity

cast meaning

Chrysoprase is the stone of prosperity and shows that a good home and lifestyle has been created, as well as financial security. The presence of chrysoprase in a cast indicates an opportunity to build on that foundation.

path forward

For the client, there may be a new business opportunity on the horizon or an ability to add to existing assets. A home could be renovated, a real estate investment made or an acquisition that may increase in value over the coming years.

outcomes

In building on an existing foundation it will be protected and the additions will add to the client's material wellbeing.

cinnabarite

merchant

cast meaning

Cinnabarite is known as the merchant's stone and indicates good outcomes in business dealings. When present with other crystals that indicate new beginnings, cinnabarite signifies new ventures, whereas crystals that represent the past signify that existing or old business can be renewed.

path forward

When cinnabarite appears in a cast, the client will be presented with an opportunity which can lead to a beneficial outcome. This is not a windfall where chance is a factor, rather a proposition where the client is able to bargain for the outcome. Bargaining is a conscious decision and involves some degree of action – the deal must involve something given in return for something received.

outcome

The outcome may not necessarily be financial but in will add to wealth in the long term.

citrine

windfall

cast meaning

Citrine is the stone of luck and fortune. It signifies an unexpected positive outcome, acquisition or gain where chance is a factor. It also indicates there are many choices available and a number of possibilities.

path forward

When citrine appears in a cast there is a prize for which the client is competing. The nature of the competition may not be known, or even the fact there is a competition, however, the outcome is surrounded by luck. While citrine indicates there will be a windfall gain, it also suggests the gain may be one of a number of possible outcomes – none of which are within the client's control. The client should be mindful of the unexpected nature of the gain and that a "win" may not indicate repetition.

outcomes

When a fortunate gain is received, it may be a one off. Gratitude will keep us from falling into the belief that a windfall, while appreciated, may not necessarily repeat. This helps us to utilize the advantage given.

clear quartz

dynamism

cast meaning

Clear quartz is a carrier of energy and indicates that things are moving around at some speed. The need here is to be aware, as apathy may lead to things being missed. This is a good time to bring plans forward or work on bringing future dreams into today's reality.

path forward

Something the client has been anticipating will, at last, happen very quickly. That does not mean it will happen tomorrow, it just means that when it does – it will be fast. The client should keep their eyes open and be on the ball or risk missing an opportunity. Clear quartz can also indicate a short-term illness or accident.

outcomes

With awareness, dreams can happen today and with focus, living in the moment will avoid disappointments and bring rewards.

clinochlore

purity

cast meaning

Clinochlore is the crystal of purity. It represents beginnings and things that are not tainted by bias and judgment. This creates cynicism which prevents positive outcomes.

path forward

When clinochlore appears in a cast, there is a matter facing the client which is clouded by the client's own preconceived ideas. These ideas may be based on previous experience which is causing an expectation of a bad outcome. The client may be living in denial of a fact. However, this is merely a mask and the client should trust that alternative outcomes are possible.

outcomes

When bias is removed, the possibility of all outcomes is acknowledged, and similar outcomes can be seen in a new light.

cobalt aura

regeneration

cast meaning

When cobalt aura appears in a cast it indicates that something has been depleted. This is usually energy and often relates to the health of the client. If unaddressed, depletion is usually replaced with eventual pain. What goes beyond just being tired, ignoring the body's demand for rest can lead to other problems. Depletion can also exist in other areas such as family bonds and finances. While this sounds negative, it is the universal call for regeneration.

path forward

The client is encouraged to put recovery first as ignoring the signs of fatigue can lead to exhaustion and greater problems. The client should also investigate what is in their life that is debilitating or causing weakness. Don't let things slip.

outcomes

There is an opportunity to regenerate and reenergize, sparking new life into things that have been waning. With proper focus, issues will subside and possibly not recur.

cordierite

decisions

cast meaning

Cordierite represents choices and will assist in making the right decisions. It helps to find a conclusion, determination or settlement where one or more choices are available. Cordierite can also indicate travel or a change in direction.

path forward

When cordierite appears in a cast, the client is facing difficult decisions. These are decisions the client may have been delaying for fear of bad judgment or bad outcomes. The lack of decision will always prevent a good outcome as much as a bad one, so in moving forward the client should view choices in a different light. Instead of seeing the finality – the "no going back" option – he/she can focus on the positives beyond the conclusion. The presence of cordierite indicates that it is time to make a choice and run with it.

outcomes

Choices are only resolved when decisions are made. Any decision will present new opportunities and views, and further choices.

dumortierite

travel

cast meaning

Dumortierite is the stone of travel and indicates a journey to be undertaken. It also relates to places and buildings, in particular places of work and study. With this combination, dumortierite often suggests moving house or changing jobs.

path forward

When dumortierite appears in a cast, the client may be considering moving house or changing jobs. In either case, this will include some travel or the travel itself may be a concern. If there are doubts or concerns about success, the client can be guided by other stones that are present. Otherwise, they may consider that going on the journey as presented will in some way be beneficial.

outcomes

The opportunity for change will only be successful if it is embraced. With travel, there are new things to be seen and learned. Keep your eyes and mind open.

epidote

addition

cast meaning

Epidote literally means addition. It signifies that a new way of looking at things will add to the path forward. Where there are choices, only one will bring something new.

path forward

The client is being presented with an opportunity to move something which is old to something which is up to date. Epidote signals there is scope for renewal and renovation. This may be in a relationship or in material things such as a home or a job promotion.

outcomes

In building upon things that already exist, the way forward will be easier than if the client adopted an "out with the old and in with the new attitude".

fuchsite

distrust

cast meaning

The appearance of fuchsite in a cast signals there are elements of betrayal and distrust surrounding a situation. This may be that a truth has yet to be revealed or that an important issue is unresolved,

path forward

The client is encouraged to examine closely why there are negative feelings and where the negative influence emanates from. This may not be the best time to move forward with plans involving major changes. Instead, the client should take smaller steps or progress slowly.

outcomes

Careful consideration, without blinkers, will lead to better chances of success.

garnet

support

cast meaning

Garnet indicates that support is available to help through painful or disruptive events. It advises that help will be useful if sought.

path forward

The client may be concerned about a particular situation that is causing some degree of pain or discomfort. In this case, the client is encouraged to seek help, particularly if the issue is physically related. Help may not come from traditional sources. Asking for support through difficult situations will bring better outcomes, even if the assistance is time given for recovery.

outcomes

Dealing with pain in a positive way increases the efficacy of rehabilitation and the speed of recovery.

girasol

fertility

cast meaning

Girasol signifies all things new and things being born. It can indicate the birth of new ideas and also of pregnancy. From birth, there is growth.

path forward

When girasol appears in a cast, the client is encouraged to try new ideas and to bring forward plans for renewal. If the client is trying for parenthood, this is a good time to take care of physical health and to address bad habits.

outcomes

When consciously moving toward renewal and accepting that all things can grow, the birth of new things brings forward joyful outcomes.

goldstone

social

cast meaning

When goldstone appears in a cast, there are social occasions in the near future which will bring both joy and the rekindling of old friendships or the making new friendships.

path forward

The client is encouraged to get out of the house and have some fun. This may be in the form of attending celebrations or just mingling with people on a non-business social level. The client should undertake classes or join with like-minded people who have similar interests or hobbies. Socialization should be done without any expectation of a specific outcome, rather just to be in the moment and to build confidence.

outcomes

Going with the flow of social involvement will build knowledge and experience.

green fluorite

equality

cast meaning

Green fluorite is the stone of equal balance. Like the justice scales, it represents equality in matters including gender, finances, life balance and so on. It represents that which is fair and reasonable, which may not always be fulfilled in equal halves. If the client is involved in a legal matter, green fluorite can signal a favorable outcome.

path forward

When green fluorite appears in a cast, the client may be grappling with a sense of inequality in a situation. The client may feel events have unfolded that appear unjust or that he/she has not received what is deserved. The client is encouraged to see both viewpoints and both sides of the scales. Often there must be some give and take to find a resolution, or compromises so that each side feels just.

outcomes

Achieving equality will involve speaking up and taking action, but will only yield success if both sides understand what is to be gained and lost, and are willing to compromise for the sake of resolution.

hematite

restriction

cast meaning

Hematite is a grounding crystal which seeks to bring matters back to their basics, to pare back the layers of clutter and negativity that prevent us from moving forward.

path forward

When hematite appears in a cast, it indicates that something is being held back or is being subject to such negativity that the client is unable to see beyond the problem. The client fails to recognize the options and choices laid out in front of them as if blinded by the current position. Hematite in a cast also signals this is a time to break free of old habits and let go of old ideas as there are new things waiting to be revealed.

outcomes

If the client sees the situation as 100% full, then there is no room for anything else. This is the time to make room, for new things are in the offing and all have potential to positively affect the outcomes.

howlite

meditation

cast meaning

Howlite is the stone of meditation, calm and peaceful harmony. Its presence signals a time to sit back and reflect, taking time out to recover from a busy life. It also encourages imagination – to picture your life, not as it is but how you want it to be. There is always room for improvement.

path forward

When howlite appears in a cast, the client is encouraged to take some time out and alleviate stress. This may mean getting together with friends and family for some overdue recreation, or just sitting down with a good book for a while. Time out can also be achieved by allowing the mind to wander, letting daydreams reveal possibilities. Howlite does not call for a complete breakaway, just to stop and take a deep breath.

outcomes

Getting away from a busy life even for a moment will help to restore energy and motivation for the next part of the journey.

hypersthene

power

cast meaning

The presence of hypersthene in a cast indicates a battle ahead. However, this battle is a conflict that is well prepared for by both sides. It is also a battle that is overdue and needs to be fought. It indicates that things are coming to a head.

path forward

The client should be confident about going into battle, especially when it is something that is desired or considered right. The issue fought for, however, must not be trivial – there must be a real and meaningful goal, not just an action that is vengeful or vexatious. However, the client should not go in blindly and must prepare for all possible outcomes. He/she may benefit from advice from elders or those who have been in similar positions, but the client should not assume that others will fight the battle for them.

outcomes

With preparedness, the outcome will be favorable. Without preparation or the right intentions, the client may be blindsided.

jadeite

release

cast meaning

When jadeite appears in a cast it indicates there is something the client is tied to that is holding back or blocking the way forward. This may be a person, emotion or past experience, or even an action that has become a negative habit.

path forward

The client is encouraged to remove his or herself from the negative influence by cutting the tie. This must be a conscious decision followed by action rather than just a wish. In the case of ties that are not physical, the cut may be performed ceremonially, however, the ceremony itself must signify an end. It may be a difficult process and make take time. The client can prepare by visualizing life after breaking free.

outcomes

When we break free of negative ties, we are free from external influences that keep us stuck in a negative situation. Energy is then allowed to flow freely and this allows us to receive positive influences such as happiness and joy.

kunzite

illumination

cast meaning

Kunzite acts like the sun, shedding light into the darkness, revealing truths and exposing things which are hidden. It also carries the energy of light which reinvigorates and replenishes as well as lifting dark veils or bringing things out of the shadows. Kunzite is strongly influenced by the female child mind and may indicate messages that come with purity, curiosity, and innocence.

path forward

When kunzite appears in a cast, the client is entering a period of happiness that is filled with light. In this state, all manner of things can be received like love, positivity, motivation and renewal. There are personal things to be revealed and at this time the client may discover previously unknown talents or may renew past talents albeit in a new light.

outcomes

With light comes openness and with openness comes knowledge. Combined together, light and knowledge allow this part of the journey to be effortless.

kyanite

partition

cast meaning

When kyanite appears in a cast it indicates two or more issues are the focus of concern. They are distinctly separate and may not be related, however, resolution of one may lead to resolution of the other/s.

path forward

The client is encouraged to deal with each issue, finding a resolution to one before moving onto the next as juggling too many at the same time will lead to delays and frustration. Focus energy on the most important problem first and persevere with it until resolved.

outcomes

Dealing with issues in an organized manner will present more options and ensure that problems only have to be dealt with once.

labradorite

visionary

cast meaning

When labradorite appears in a cast it signifies the increase of knowledge gained through the sharing of ideas. It also indicates the formation of a future business partnership or of a future marriage.

path forward

The client may be considering entering into a new partnership which demands a high degree of collaboration. The success of the partnership will be determined by how much the parties are able or willing to contribute to the goal. In business, the client should ensure that the intended partner provides something tangible other than just their support or presence. In marriage, the client should acknowledge that both partners equally share the responsibility for success.

outcomes

With a strong commitment to collaboration and the marriage of minds, the way forward will lead to prosperity.

lapis lazuli

ancestors

cast meaning

Lapis lazuli is the stone of belonging and is representative of all things in the past, especially family ties. When it appears in a cast it signifies that today's events are strongly based on historical factors and influenced by things that are already known.

path forward

The client is encouraged to look back, as his/her history already has the answers. They have simply been overlooked or forgotten. A memory of having "been here before" means something in the past can provide the information or experience that can help the client today if only to explain why things are the way they are. If the client feels disconnected in some way then looking back will help to develop a stronger sense of belonging.

outcomes

Family ties will be stronger and better understood. The value of relationships will be enhanced, leading to a decreased feeling of isolation. Draw on the knowledge of the past to better connect to today.

lepidolite

deadlock

cast meaning

When lepidolite appears in a cast it indicates that a deadlock has occurred in a situation. When this prevents forward movement it hinders the ability to grow and may result in a standoff or a complete stalemate.

path forward

To break a stalemate, the client is encouraged to look beyond the problem, allowing imagination to show how the situation could be improved. What will things look like if the barrier of deadlock is broken? Can a stalemate be resolved by working together to find acceptable compromises? In some cases, the client may have to sit things through and wait until the storm has passed, in which case the client should focus attention on other things.

outcomes

Sometimes, removing barriers may involve some compromises which may not seem ideal, however, it may be worth it in the long run.

magnesite

attraction

cast meaning

Magnesite is the stone of attraction, however, this is attraction must be tempered with respect. It means a desire to attract things into life must not come with a view of gluttony or excessiveness, or to the detriment of others. Abundance comes only when the outcome is received with gratitude.

path forward

When magnesite appears in a cast, the client is encouraged to actively seek out the things that he/she desires. Sitting back, waiting for things to happen will result in the status quo. The client needs to be clear about what they want. In the search, the client must do so with respect, and anything received must be reciprocated with gratitude. Likewise, anything given in return must be done so unconditionally.

outcomes

Attraction is underpinned with both kindness and gratitude and there is always a way to show both, no matter how small. Often the only cost is self-sacrifice. If the thing received is not treated as valued, then it will indeed be valueless.

malachite

settlement

cast meaning

Malachite represents a settlement of an issue by way of reaching an agreement, or a turnaround in a situation based upon a decision being made. Either way, the resolution is final.

path forward

When malachite appears in a cast the client may be faced with choices upon which a decision must be made. When many choices are apparent, this can be overwhelming which can lead to no decision being made at all. The client should investigate if there is room for negotiation, however, at some point, a decision must be made. This may be regarded as a firm commitment or as a leap of faith. Either way, the client should view the settlement as the removal of a barrier to the way forward.

outcomes

Any decision made will present new opportunities and views, and further choices, and it is only after the settlement that new decisions will be available.

mookaite

patriarch

cast meaning

Mookaite represents male energies. This is most likely a person, however, it can also be any influence that is sensed as orderly, logical or fatherly. It represents practical values which are not governed by emotions.

path forward

The presence of mookaite in a cast suggests the client can look to a strong male influence for guidance. Most likely in a professional environment, this influence or person can help to reveal things as they really are, rather than how you imagine them to be. In a personal relationship, the male influence will help to retain order and keep the relationship grounded.

outcomes

When relationships or activities are conflicted, or when the nature of a bond is uncertain, a male influence will help to balance emotions with a calm logical order.

moss agate

connection

cast meaning

Moss agate is the stone of connection. It represents things we are drawn to for no apparent reason.

path forward

When moss agate appears in a cast, the client is encouraged to follow the path that is becoming available in front – there are things to be gained or messages to hear. If the client has been contemplating a change, such as starting a new hobby or taking a course, moss agate is signaling that this is the right time to commence.

outcomes

When drawn to something it is best not to ignore it as the universe if guiding us to a new part of life.

nuummite

alchemy

cast meaning

Nuummite is the stone of transformation, helping to visualize hopes and ideals. It helps to distinguish between what is possible and what is unrealistic using the available means.

path forward

When nuummite appears in a cast, it signifies that all of the tools necessary to make life changes are available to the client, however perhaps he/she is failing to recognize them or to put them to use. This may be as simple as using existing knowledge to better a bad situation, or to transform hopes into reality. The client is encouraged to investigate what is holding them back.

outcomes

Asking "what do I need to make this happen?" and then positioning oneself to believe it can happen will transform dreams into reality. It is time to stop dreaming and start doing.

optical calcite

mastery

cast meaning

Optical calcite is the master's stone and it governs understanding and finding solutions to complex problems, such that any task can be mastered with ease. It is particularly relevant to any client considering or undertaking academic study.

path forward

When optical calcite appears in a cast, the client is encouraged to do some study which may be as simple as taking a course or reading up on a subject of interest. In this case, the client's experience is not sufficient to unravel the answers to complex problems and knowledge will be gained through further investigation.

outcomes

Understand or perceiving unfamiliar ideas will be helped when realizing that there is always more to learn.

orange calcite

recognition

cast meaning

When optical calcite appears in a cast it indicates that recognition for hard work has not yet been attained. This may be in a job, especially where the recognition of others is causing resentment. It may also be in special activities where natural talent appears underappreciated or underutilized.

path forward

The client may be feeling underappreciated for the efforts he/she is making in an activity. Or, they may feel that tasks undertaken are menial and undervalued, without regard to their experience or talent. In this case, the client is encouraged to speak up and put forward a case for acknowledgment. Some self-promotion is warranted as often the only one feeling worthless is the client. The appreciation is likely there – it is just not being conveyed.

outcomes

When recognition for hard work is absent, there will be hesitation to undertake or complete further tasks. When hesitation is broken we are able to move forward.

orange selenite

solstice

cast meaning

Orange selenite is commonly called moonstone and it governs anything that is periodic in nature. This can be times where specific things happen such as religious events or anniversaries, or periods where tasks are commonly repeated such as book work, or meetings.

path forward

When orange selenite appears in a cast it signifies one of two things. The client may be apprehensive about an upcoming event or the client feeling as though he/she is in a rut and that things have become too routine. In the first case, the client is encouraged to give anxiety to the universe as what will be, will be. The event will pass and it is better to dispel fear for what is inevitable. In the second case, the client is encouraged to make positive changes, to mix things up a little without trashing the task at hand. This is a time to take stock of the situation.

outcomes

As we feather our nest, life is bound to become cyclical. When anxiety or boredom set in, this is a time to find new ways of doing the same thing.

peridot

happiness

cast meaning

Peridot is the stone of happiness. It signifies joy on both a physical and spiritual level. In crystal work, the spirit is naturally in constant pursuit of happiness and its only barrier to joy being the barriers that are self-imposed.

path forward

When peridot appears in a cast, the client is entering a new phase of happiness where feelings of sadness, isolation, and melancholy are lifted. However, this will be hindered if the client places obstacles in the way. In this new phase, the client will be offered ways to expose hidden gifts and talents. It is a time that he/she will be allowed to tap into the soul to reveal the authentic self. The client is encouraged to take the bull by the horns and run with it, lifting the veil of apathy.

outcomes

Maintaining a state of happiness means being open to whatever may come. It always helps to deliver good outcomes. This is a moment to see the glass as half full and to revel in offered optimism.

pietersite

elders

cast meaning

Pietersite represents the wisdom and experience of elders, both male and female. While pietersite is likely to represent a person who has influence over the client, it can also mean a male or female energy, being either practical or creative.

path forward

When pietersite appears in a cast the client is encouraged to look to elders for guidance in a particular situation. If the cause of concern is grounded in practicality or logic this will be an older male influence or if derived from growth and creativity then an older female influence. For example, if the client is concerned about finances then this is grounded in practicality (male) whereas if the client is concerned about love, then this is grounded in creativity (female). The client should be aware that the actual gender of the elder is often non-specific. An older woman may be able to provide logical guidance and so forth.

outcomes

Guidance derived from grounded experience and knowledge will lead to better understanding and more positive outcomes.

pink calcite

river

cast meaning

Pink calcite governs all areas of friendship. When it appears in a cast it signifies relationships that have soured or friendships that have been broken. This may not be with a particular person but can also relate to groups, interests, and activities.

path forward

The cast is stating that in order to move forward there must be acceptance of past events. Wrongs can't be made right, there is no way to go back. It is what it is. The client is encouraged to go with the flow for now as the path forward is the only way to heal wounds. Now is not the time to try and fix things. The client should focus attention on other matters that bring joy such that when the time is right, mending is undertaken in the right light.

outcomes

Mending a broken relationship can only be done where the intent is without blame and free from shadows of the past. Time will reveal the light into which the hurt can be dissolved.

purple fluorite

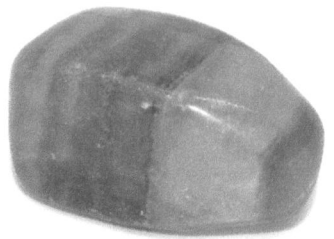

intensity

cast meaning

When purple fluorite appears in a cast it signals excitement and the possibility of news ahead. At the same time, the pace of life will intensify.

path forward

The client is encouraged to approach the immediate future with some degree of optimism and enthusiasm as there are signs of good things to come. This does not mean to abandon the current path in expectation, but to prepare for a busy schedule ahead. New opportunities will arise which, when harnessed, will emerge as a positive force.

outcomes

Setting aside time to focus on this new development will bring rewards in the longer term.

pyrite

change

cast meaning

Pyrite is known as fool's gold and it is a powerful generator of change. Due to its mineral content, pyrite is unstable and in nature, it is constantly being reformed. In a cast, pyrite can be interpreted as a situation that is constantly changing, new things are being revealed, and old things are being transformed.

path forward

The client is experiencing a time of great change both in their circumstances and in their thinking. While this may be uncomfortable and confusing for now, there is a process that change must go through before things settle down. The client should embrace the process – not everything will be bad as from change always emerges new ideas, new opportunities, and new enthusiasm.

outcomes

In trusting the process of change, truth and authenticity will be revealed, providing a solid base for the next phase of life. Go with the flow for now, and enjoy the ride!

red jasper

matriarch

cast meaning

Red jasper is the stone of all things feminine. It governs emotions, nurture, and nature, as well as fertility, bonding, and creativity.

path forward

When red jasper appears in a cast it encourages the client to develop the female hemisphere of their personality. This may mean starting a new creative process from which things can grow or attune with nature on a more practical level. Often red jasper indicates the client would benefit from working on spirituality to a greater degree.

outcomes

When growth is experienced from its earliest beginnings we become open to the idea that all things are able to be expanded and developed, such that positivity can be drawn from the process.

rhodochrosite

defeat

cast meaning

Rhodochrosite is the stone of defeat. This does not mean that something is lost but does indicate that starting over will yield good outcomes.

path forward

When rhodochrosite appears in a cast, it signifies that a situation has run its course, served its purpose and is no longer useful. The client will be rewarded by letting go and focusing on future paths, especially if the matter has been the subject of obsession.

outcomes

When something is no longer useful or relevant, it is time to move forward.

rhodonite

anxiety

cast meaning

When rhodonite appears in a cast it represents some degree of apprehension is felt over a situation which has been disruptive and uncomfortable. It may have caused considerable anger or animosity leading to insecurity and isolation. Rhodonite, however, signals a way forward.

path forward

If the client continues to dwell on a past negative experience, then he/she will only attract more negativity and the problem will not be resolved. In fact, a negative attitude will permeate into other areas of life. The client is encouraged to set aside the issues that surround the situation and to focus on the positives.

outcomes

When negativity develops into fear and anxiety, the ability to move forward in a positive way is hindered. Now is the time to push through, find peace and heal old wounds.

rose quartz

heart

cast meaning

Rose quartz is the stone of the heart. It governs how we feel about one another, how we treat each other, and how we relate to the world around. It signifies that the choice of love is available and real, on any level.

path forward

When rose quartz appears in a cast it means the client has true love surrounding a situation, beyond friendships or likes. It signifies duality, the meeting of two minds to become one, in which a choice is being presented. The client must decide to either follow their heart or to take a different route.

outcomes

When the heart is followed, it does not guarantee a road paved with gold. The experience of love itself must outweigh any negatives.

sardonyx

philosopher

cast meaning

Sardonyx is the universal stone of understanding, governing many areas including awareness and living a conscious life. It signifies higher versions of education, intelligence, wisdom, and knowledge.

path forward

When sardonyx appears in a cast, the client is encouraged to undertake some higher learning on any subject in which the client is interested. This may be done in a traditional academic sense but may study also relate to spirituality or more philosophical ideas. Sardonyx encourages the strengthening of beliefs through both education and experience.

outcomes

In the pursuit of wisdom, the outcome is not necessarily a qualification written on paper. Often the outcome is a greater understanding of the journey.

scolecite

singularity

cast meaning

Scolecite is the stone of singles. It can signify a one-off event or an object that is received just for one purpose or use. It can also represent first-time success depending on other crystals present.

path forward

When scolecite appears in a cast, the client may have an upcoming event that is special and never to be repeated. In this case, the client is encouraged to bath in the light it brings for it may be fleeting although memorable. Also, scolecite may indicate that the client is juggling too many issues at the same time which may cause things to slip through the cracks.

outcomes

A single moment in time can make a longer lasting memory than a repeated experience.

serpentine

negativity

cast meaning

While serpentine represents negativity, it also serves as a warning sign that an attitude or influence needs to be cleared such that positivity is not repelled in the outcome. Consider it snake-like, as negativity has a tendency to bend and twist, it takes keeping eyes open to prevent it from lashing out and biting.

path forward

When serpentine appears in a cast, the client may be dealing with a problem that is surrounded by a negative influence. In this case, the client should be aware that if left unchecked, this influence will snake its way through to other areas. It is best to address the source of the negativity early and get to the bottom of difficult problems before it devours all things in its path.

outcomes

To avoid destruction, remain vigilant. Keep paths open for positive influence and to repel the effects of negativity.

shungite

contentment

cast meaning

Shungite is the stone of content. It represents wishes fulfilled and dreams realized. While this is always a joyful outcome, it can be short-lived if further plans are not made.

path forward

When shungite appears in a cast, the client is encouraged to look forward to the realization of things for which he/she has been striving to achieve. It is both the payoff for hard work and the delivery of just deserves. The client should enjoy the process of just "doing" for a while, basking in the success, however, the shine will wane if the client does not take the opportunity to make further plans or enhancements.

outcomes

While achievement brings contentment, there is more to be gained by drawing on the power of success.

smoky quartz

action

cast meaning

When smoky quartz appears in a cast it indicates a situation that needs attention. If left unattended problems will arise and permeate into other areas, or a possible advantage will be missed.

path forward

The client may have been putting off doing a particular task because it either seems trivial or appears insurmountable. Either way, the time has come to be assertive and take action. If the task requires a lot of energy then the client will be rewarded with further advantages and more opportunities once the situation is cleared.

outcomes

Once the action is commenced, the horizon will emerge revealing new opportunities.

snowflake obsidian

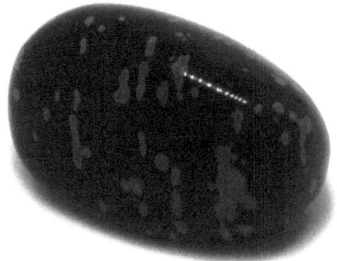

speed

cast meaning

Snowflake obsidian represents speed. It signifies a quickening of pace in the events surrounding situations making for a busy period ahead.

path forward

When snowflake obsidian appears in a cast, the client is encouraged to deal with issues quickly and to be careful not to make hasty judgments. This is also a time to break some bad habits as these will hold back the process of change.

outcomes

Go with what feels right at the time so as to prevent creating mountains out of molehills.

sodalite

collaboration

cast meaning

Sodalite represents a gathering of minds that share information. In a cast, it indicates that help is available, although it has not yet been sought or asked for. Help may come in the form of assistance from another person or insights into how other similar events have evolved. Help may also consist of education wherein simply researching the issue may provide answers.

path forward

The client should ask for help with a particular issue. Look to others that have similar experience or expertise, and seek to collaborate, rather than just looking for someone else to solve it. The client needs to be an active participant in the solution.

outcomes

With knowledge, the client will be empowered to deal with a situation and to act positively, with some reasonable expectation of the result.

sunstone

advancement

cast meaning

Sunstone is the crystal of advancement. It signifies good outcomes when conscious endeavors are made to get ahead, particularly in business.

path forward

When sunstone appears in a cast, the client is encouraged to take action to move things forward in business. This is a time to do some marketing and focus on sales as the groundwork has already been set for advancement. Move ahead with enthusiasm and take a winning attitude. Accept any constructive criticism as it comes from those who are willing to negotiate in order to achieve the perfect outcome.

outcomes

As each new day dawns, new avenues emerge for advancement. They just need to be explored.

tiger's eye

perfection

cast meaning

Tiger's eye is the stone of perfection and represents ideals and goals. It is highly governed by the logical mind which seeks to find order as the smoothest path forward.

path forward

When tiger's eye appear in a cast, the client is encouraged to pursue goals as this is a time for achievement. However, if there are loose ends or past unresolved issues, these need to be addressed as they will create barriers on the path forward. There is a natural order which should be followed.

outcomes

Natural idealism says that all things can be helped in some way, no matter how seemingly perfect. Even perfection must be maintained.

turquoise

health

cast meaning
Turquoise is the most highly prized of the ancient crystals and it governs all matters relating to health.

path forward
When turquoise appears in a cast, the surrounding stones will indicate which part of the client's life needs to be focused on such as to prevent that part becoming stale or falling into sickness. Turquoise can also stand as a warning bell for possible physical health and the client is encouraged to take some time to eliminate damaging influences. It also indicates a positive time to achieve weight and fitness goals.

outcomes
When the body or spirit calls for rest or recovery, it is best to heed the warnings.

unakite

security

cast meaning
As the stone of security, unakite protects from negative influence and also from loss. It wards against the effects of risk taking in the material world, and of harm from negative people in the physical world.

path forward
When unakite appears in a cast, the client is encouraged to keep their eyes open to possible threats. In recognizing vulnerability, the client will be better positioned to protect the things he/she holds dear. While hazards may be unavoidable and beyond the control of the client, there are simple measures that can be taken to avoid harm. This does not mean the client should lock his or herself away or be obsessive, just to be watchful.

outcomes
When hard work and perseverance has provided prosperity, the next task is ensuring those benefits remain. Be vigilant and stand the ground.

vulcanite

hope

cast meaning

Vulcanite represents hope and exuberance. It is highly influenced by karma and says that energy projected outwardly will be received in kind.

path forward

When vulcanite appears in a cast, the client is encouraged to adopt a positive approach to life matters. It will be beneficial to accept that "whatever will be, will be" however there is much that can be done to influence the way the outcome is received and perceived. Expecting a negative result will result in just that – no matter whether the outcome is good or bad.

outcomes

Putting forward positivity will allow the outcome to be received in a way that it is always perceived as beneficial in some way. We get what we ask for.

white selenite

celebration

cast meaning

White selenite is the stone of celebration. It signals there are good times ahead and that it is time to play. Social occasions involving family and friends will be humorous and light hearted.

path forward

When white selenite appears in a cast, the client is encouraged to have some fun and don't take things too seriously. It's a good time to be around children or those that are young at heart.

outcomes

When spirits are lifted by youthful thoughts, the way forward is a journey of discovery.

yellow opal

transformation

cast meaning

Yellow opal is the stone of endings and transformation, signaling that a new turn or opportunity is sought or on the horizon. If transformation was not intended, the sudden change can be unsettling at first.

path forward

When yellow opal appears in a cast, the client may see the end of a troubling situation. With this, the client is encouraged to not dwell on the past but to seize the opportunity move forward. This is a time of renewal and regeneration and there are new directions that were previously unavailable. Some unpredicted change is fortuitous.

outcomes

Transformation is only beneficial when we look to the forward path that transformation brings. There is no reason to look back.

crystal categories

clearing	agate	malachite	sardonyx
	apatite	optical calcite	serpentine
	black obsidian	orange calcite	sodalite
	cordierite	pink calcite	vulcanite
	jadeite	rhodonite	white selenite
energizing	amazonite	clear quartz	nuummite
	amethyst	clinochlore	orange selenite
	aquamarine	epidote	peridot
	black onyx	girasol	pietersite
	blue fluorite	goldstone	purple fluorite
	blue quartz	green fluorite	pyrite
	bronzite	hypersthene	red jasper
	carnelian	kunzite	rose quartz
	chalcedony	kyanite	smoky quartz
	cinnabarite	magnesite	snowflake obsidian
	citrine	mookaite	sunstone
grounding	ametrine	labradorite	scolecite
	aventurine	lapis lazuli	tiger's eye
	garnet	lepidolite	yellow opal
	hematite	moss agate	
protecting	chrysoprase	fuchsite	shungite
	cobalt aura	howlite	turquoise
	dumortierite	rhodochrosite	unakite

crystals a-z

agate	advantage	clear quartz	dynamism
amazonite	self-reliance	clinochlore	purity
amethyst	creation	cobalt aura	regeneration
ametrine	middle ground	cordierite	decisions
apatite	revelation	dumortierite	travel
aquamarine	sixth sense	epidote	addition
aventurine	triumph	fuchsite	distrust
black obsidian	courage	garnet	support
black onyx	pilgrimage	girasol	fertility
blue fluorite	interlude	goldstone	social
blue quartz	comfort	green fluorite	equality
bronzite	fortitude	hematite	restriction
carnelian	acrimony	howlite	meditation
chalcedony	intellect	hypersthene	power
chrysoprase	prosperity	jadeite	release
cinnabarite	merchant	kunzite	illumination
citrine	windfall	kyanite	partition

labradorite	visionary	rhodochrosite	defeat
lapis lazuli	ancestors	rhodonite	anxiety
lepidolite	deadlock	rose quartz	heart
magnesite	attraction	sardonyx	philosopher
malachite	settlement	scolecite	singularity
mookaite	patriarch	serpentine	negativity
moss agate	connection	shungite	contentment
nuummite	alchemy	smoky quartz	action
optical calcite	mastery	snowflake obsidian	speed
orange calcite	recognition	sodalite	collaboration
orange selenite	solstice	sunstone	advancement
peridot	happiness	tiger's eye	perfection
pietersite	elders	turquoise	health
pink calcite	river	unakite	security
purple fluorite	intensity	vulcanite	hope
pyrite	change	white selenite	celebration
red jasper	matriarch	yellow opal	transformation

astrological crystals

aquarius	Jan 21 – Feb 19	garnet
pisces	Feb 20 – Mar 20	amethyst
aries	Mar 21 – Apr 20	unakite
taurus	Apr 21 – May 21	aura cobalt
gemini	May 22 – Jun 21	agate
cancer	Jun 22 – Jul 23	peridot
leo	Jul 24 – Aug 23	black onyx
virgo	Aug 24 – Sep 23	carnelian
libra	Sep 24 – Oct 23	apatite
scorpio	Oct 24 – Nov 22	aquamarine
sagittarius	Nov 23 – Dec 21	clear quartz
capricorn	Dec 22 – Jan 20	red jasper

www.ingramcontent.com/pod-product-compliance
Lightning Source LLC
Chambersburg PA
CBHW042051290426
44110CB00001B/23